Learning from an Unimportant Minority

Race Politics Beyond the White/Black Paradigm

J. Sakai

KER
SPL
EBE
DEB
2015

Learning from an Unimportant Minority
ISBN: 978-1-894946-60-5

Copyright 2015 J. Sakai
This edition copyright 2015 Kersplebedeb

Kersplebedeb Publishing
CP 63560
CCCP Van Horne
Montreal, Quebec
Canada H3W 3H8

email: info@kersplebedeb.com
web: www.kersplebedeb.com
        www.leftwingbooks.net

Copies available from AK Press: www. akpress.org

Printed in canada

ACKNOWLEDGEMENT

This is based on an informal talk given on May 26, 2014, in Montreal, as part of Festival of Anarchy. My thanks to Dale, not simply for transcribing this talk and talks before this, but for his skill at raising blurred phrases and confused discussion back into clear wording for the reader.

LEARNING FROM AN UNIMPORTANT MINORITY

Race politics beyond the official white/black paradigm

a talk with J. Sakai

QPIRG Concordia
1500 de Maisonneuve W., rm. 204

Monday, May 26 at 6:30 pm

wheelchair accessible

traduction chuchoté
versle français

got questions?
info@kersplebedeb.com

RACE IS NOTORIOUSLY SLIPPERY, awkward to hold onto as a subject, yet totally all around us. Totally. All the time, every day, we breathe it; *after all, it is us*, so we can't ever be far from it. This seeming contradiction of what should be so simple being endlessly complicated in society is because how we think about race, how we talk about race … capitalism is constantly trying to police this. They don't want to neaten it, they actually want to constrict it and keep remaking it in their own distorted images and stamping it on our faces.

So in u.s. society—i'm not talking about any other country because that's not my experience—in u.s. society, capitalism pushes thinking and talking about race into the dominant form of a white/Black paradigm. Where everything is supposed to be arranged according to the relationship between white men—who are defined as: What's "normal", the standard—and New Afrikan people—who are indirectly or covertly depicted as incomplete or deficient models of the first. So that the supposed goal of capitalistic "antiracism" is that eventually at some point everyone will be exactly like white men.

Well, we don't have to comment really on that.

Into this paradigm, everyone else—"unimportant minorities"—are essentially crammed and flattened into that two-dimensional story, according to some always shifting order that they have, judging by how important or unimportant they think we are.

This raises a question: What is an unimportant minority? Am not going to answer that, but let me point you in a certain direction.

IN 2007 IN **CHICAGO ON A SPRING EVENING,** a young white man was walking along the lakefront, Lake Michigan, and he saw an Asian fisherman, alone. Well, seeing his opportunity he charged this fisherman from behind, attacked him, started pummeling him, and managed to throw him into the water. And this fisherman, Mr. Duan, a Vietnamese, died, drowned. Getting the idea that he might be in trouble, the young white man took off. But he didn't make it very far before the police caught him.

Eyewitnesses coming forward, other people coming forward, and a minimal amount of investigation soon revealed that in at least two other incidents in the preceding weeks, this white guy had attacked Asian fishermen who he caught alone at night on the rocks by the lake. One man was beaten and thrown into the water but managed to swim away to safety. Another man actually had some martial arts training and fought this guy off and the guy took off running full speed, so that worked out okay.

Well, this looks really obvious, right? Next day all the newspapers, the politicians, everybody's onboard. These are terrible hate crimes. This guy's a racist. He's a murderer. He's committing hate crimes. Definitely, this is a top priority. The FBI investigates, the homicide department, the prosecution, everybody's involved. Because they're out to defend us, as they keep telling us.

Okay, that's until they get to court where this young white guy and his lawyers stand up and say, "Actually, you have it all wrong. I'm not a racist. Point 1: Because I'm an antiracist skinhead and I have a membership card in an organization that shows this. Secondly, I wasn't committing any hate crimes because on that night I wasn't alone. I was accompanied by a white woman and my friend who is a black man. So we're completely diverse. So it can't be a hate crime because we are diverse, and I am a member of an organization that is completely against killing Black people only Asians. I'm sorry about killing that unimportant man, you know, I just got a little rowdy. You know how it is, you're young and you try and work off your energy and … you know how it goes, I didn't mean to kill anybody … these things just happen."

Well, this was a big shock! Pow! Right to the politicians' public relations guts! 'Cause what he said really made a lot of sense when viewed through the mass spectrum whiteoscope that America uses to see things by. The FBI was investigating, the federal government comes in, the human rights commission comes in. You know, everyone's investigating. Finally they go to court again and they say, *"He's right. We investigated and everything he says is true. He can't be a racist because he belongs to an antiracist organization, and these can't be hate crimes because he was accompanied by a white woman and a black man who diversified him."*

So recreationally attacking and killing Asians is not a hate crime here. Because our identity is overruled by the more important identities of a white woman and a Black man. To say nothing of the civil rights platinum card that all white men possess. Killing us isn't any hateful something or other. All of a sudden the murder charge is dropped, his lawyer and the judges agree he'll be guilty of manslaughter because he did kill somebody, even if he was only an unimportant Asian, and he'll have to serve 10 years in prison minus if he keeps his nose clean the good time served. Whatever. In other words, 5 years or so he's out.

Okay, that gives you a rough idea what an unimportant minority is.

NOW IN REAL LIFE THERE ARE NO UNIMPORTANT MINORITIES, from our point of view. I mean not just for the normal very basic reason that the human race is a mosaic composed of an unbelievable number of parts and diversity which we don't fully understand except that we need it all. But the more immediate and pragmatic reason is: You can't understand race by using the official white/Black paradigm—where everything is arranged according to that relationship—any more than you can locate something using just one dimension. i mean, when surveyors map a terrain, they triangulate, they view mountains, rivers, whatever from different angles of perspective to triangulate the location of these things. Realistically that's what we need. So, in that sense, it isn't just that there are no unimportant peoples, it's that we need to find all those other angles of experience and perspective.

One thing, a little "p.s.": When i say a white/Black paradigm, I don't mean that's the only thing, so to speak, on capitalism's mind. That's not true, obviously, in terms of race. Because any time there's an oppressed population of any density or size—in america anyway—in or near anything that the European settler population wants or wants to control, it's like a black hole bending waves of gravity, that population becomes temporarily or locally intensely important. This is just obvious.

This is something i didn't understand, growing up in Chicago, where race is kind of stark and not complicated at all. But during Wounded Knee II ... i don't know if people know about it? It was the Indigenous ... the Indian takeover of the Pine Ridge Reservation, the Lakota Sioux Reservation, in 1973, in South Dakota where they were then surrounded by the Army and the FBI and police and they stood them off for 71 days ... well, this was a major thing in u.s. history actually and i'd like to say that the movement responded with this tremendous heroic effort. But actually we were too tied up in our own work and messed up half the time to do those kind of things if we didn't have any real advance notice. And we didn't have any advance notice then.

So, i was at home thinking, "Yeah, we're going to have to go to that demonstration, but when is it anyway? We all know there's got to be one to support the struggle of Pine Ridge, you know?" We got a call from the support committee. The left support in 1973 in the united states for Indigenous struggles was sentimentally there, but very thin on the ground since they were judged a righteous but unimportant minority. In Chicago it's only a small support committee. They call up, they say, "We just spoke to the brothers on the reservation. Whatever you do, don't come. We know people want to come. Don't do it. The big problem they have is they don't need more people. They're under siege. They're having trouble feeding the people they have. So don't come and just add extra people they have to take care of." We said, "Oh, okay," then we started to ask, "Well, when's the support demonstration?" but they'd hung up the phone.

Turns out they hung up the phone, packed their bags and put them in the trunk of their car, drove right off that night to South Dakota because, unlike what they'd told us, they wanted to be in the action too just like we would have. So there we were like, "What do we do?" We didn't know.

Anyways, so a couple of weeks later, i said, okay, like, that's it, i'm supposed to take my summer vacation— and I'm taking it.

So a friend of mine and me, we got in the old car, we're driving to San Francisco. You know, to chill out, go to the Golden Gate Bridge, all that stuff. So we're driving and real coincidently, and this was literally out of my mind, not thinking about this, we're driving through, i don't know, South Dakota, or we were near South Dakota anyway. So we stop at a large diner right by the highway. i mean really large, cuz it's the kind of place where buses stop and unload so everybody can buy overpriced hamburgers. And so we stop and walk in and sit down and we're looking around and then the guy who's sitting down next to us, he's looking at us, he gets up. Picks up his cup of coffee, picks up his plate of food, walks all the way across the dining room and sits on the other side.

"Whoa! i guess they really hate Japanese here!" i can't figure this out. You know, i don't remember us attacking South Dakota in World War II. And sure enough all the other white people around us, they're all looking at each other, they all get up, grab their cokes, their coffees, their plates of food and they all move over to the other side, far away from us. The two of us are just sitting there, like, what is going on, you know? So then the waitress comes and she is clearly freaked out. I mean she is almost running and she gets about ten feet away from us and she throws a big plastic-covered menu on our table and runs away. Turns around and runs away, all the way to the back of the restaurant. i hear her screaming at the manager. He's talking she's screaming. i hear them, rarara. And i'm saying, "What the fuck is this? Haven't these people ever seen a Japanese before?! What did we do?!"

The manager comes out and he's kind of stammering, "I'm sorry, but uh uh uh"—and he disappears! What the hell is this!? Finally my friend says, "Oh my God!" He says, "They think you're Indian!" i said "What?" And then it hits me: i'm wearing denim work clothes, boots, i had a real suntan because i've been out in the sun a lot, and that was when i was younger so still had hair, long black hair growing down below my shoulders. Oh my God, they think i'm a native warrior come to attack them and they're running! "Okay," I said, "we're going to go to another restaurant. i can't take this. This is too surreal." i don't feel insulted, i just feel like it's surreal—white people just having this momentary delusional fantasy and i'm accidentally caught in the middle of it. (Usually they just do it with themselves and i don't notice.)

I'**M GOING TO TALK ABOUT AS AN EXAMPLE,** the only one i have. What i mean by the different angle i have of experience and vision to understand race is using Japanese-americans because that's what i am and it's hard to do somebody else's i think. And i have to put in a disclaimer. This is not an "Asian-american history". i don't know that much about that. i just use some of the furniture from those rooms as props and it absolutely does not represent the Japanese-american community which would completely freak out if they found out that i was saying half these things. i'm probably not even a member in good standing. i don't have a membership card anymore. And i don't even speak Japanese since i got broken of that as a young kid at the end of World War II.

The first thing is that, to start with, there is something really unfortunately unique about us. We didn't ask for it, it came with us. It's that we're the only people of color in the united states, or to my knowledge in North America, that where our people originally came from unfortunately happens to be a really aggressive and unpleasant imperialist capitalist power. So people all over the world are none too fond of Japanese. And for good reasons or bad reasons, well here we are—i'd like to be somebody else some days, but there it is.

i had a friend who'd actually never been to Asia and he went to Japan on a vacation and he came back raving about how beautiful and wonderful it was, how civilized and peaceful, how it was a better society and all this. And i said, "Uh, you got the propaganda tour, i can tell that. You probably had Japanese friends tell you all this shit."

There's this thing. There's this fight going on right now. It's about ... Everybody's heard of Hiroshima, and the holy ground in effect, the ground zero, the shrine where the original building ... the space where the first atom bomb was dropped on a human population ... which is, you know, almost a sacred place, and it should be. Right at the edge of that is a very small memorial; it's to the dogs who died at Hiroshima that day. Nothing wrong with that, i'm a dog person myself. i like dogs.

But since there's that little monument there, a little memorial to the dogs who died, the Korean Survivors Association—the association of forced Korean laborers who were at Hiroshima that day—who've been requesting that they too be allowed to put up a memorial there, said: "We've been asking basically our entire lives for this little recognition for our people, so that we have some place at the site to come to and remember that day. You put one up for your dogs, so how about us? How can you say no to us?" Answer: *No!* Well that's one of the qualities that make Japan as a nation and as an imperialist power so loved throughout Asia. Can't say any more than that.

Actually, i didn't realize myself—not being over there, being here—just how hated we were, until the tsunami a couple years ago with the Fukushima nuclear plant and everything. Yeah, that was an interesting experience. Like the Chinese woman who came up and said, "Oh, is your family okay? Was anybody hurt?" What i've learned is that they have to ask that because if you say to them, "Ah, yeah we were just outside the Fukushima nuclear reactor and now my whole family is glowing in the dark" … well then they can't tee off on you, you see. So they have to ask that first. So i said, "Oh no, my family was in Tokyo, not that i know them anymore, you know, and nobody's hurt. They're fine." So the woman looks relieved, stands a little straighter, and says, *"You know, a lot more people were killed at the rape of Nanking."* Turns around and walks away. Well of course that's true. That's just the facts, historical fact.

Then there's the Pakistani guy who works at the Muslim laundromat i go to. He's kind of retired now, he's in the states living with his children, but he spent his working life as a seaman, a merchant seaman aboard small freighters on the Karachi-Yokohama cargo route. So he spent a lot of time in Japan over the years and we have a talking friendly acquaintance or whatever. He comes up, "Is your family okay? Is anybody hurt?" And I said, "No no no, everybody's okay"—and i'm thinking i should back away, i don't know what's going to happen. *"You Japanese,"* he says, *"you only take care of yourselves, isn't that right?"* And he turns around, he walks away. So i'm thinking, this is my lucky day obviously, you know. Good thing i'm not going to drive or buy a lottery ticket today, 'cause that all won't work out, i know that.

And some people have heard about the misspeaks of people like Cappie Pondexter. She's the all-star guard on the New York Liberty women's pro basketball team. She's the one who Twittered after the tsunami: *"What if god was tired of the way they treat their own people in there own country! Idk guys he makes no mistakes."* Later she added: *"u just never know! They did Pearl Harbor so u can't expect anything less..."* Under pressure from team and league officials, Pondexter pretended to apologize, writing: *"I didn't realize that my words could be interpreted in the manner which they were."* Yeah, sure.

So, i have to give you a little capsule, a little bit of history, boring history, and i'll try to do it the american way, we'll wrap it in a little bit of Hollywood movie lore. The way we understand the real world.

As a people, the Japanese-americans came over at the beginning of the 20th century. Mostly, in the beginning, we came over in contract labor gangs to help the railroads lay out the tracks. My grandfather came over with such a gang in 1902. Gradually that expanded. Contract labor gangs worked for large farms doing farm labor. That kind of thing. We weren't an urban people, particularly, and we did not have skilled jobs or any of that kind of stuff. We were blue-collar labor, that's what we were doing here. This is a very familiar immigrant story.

But in 1905 something happened that changed that equation somewhat. Which is that Japan defeated Russia in the war of 1905. Took Manchuria with its mineral and industrial resources, and for the first time one of the major western powers had been militarily defeated by the newly constructed armies and navies of some other emerging power. Japan announced its entrance into the war of the great powers; it became an ally in World War I and reached the rank of being able to take part officially, not unofficially—unofficially is where they have the war on top of you, officially is where you're supposedly one of the combatants—so officially it got to be of the big boys in World War I.

That triggered this shockwave of cultural hatred in the united states. Japanese were treacherous, untrustworthy, they wanted to sneakily absorb the knowledge they had gotten from their friendly European and american, you know, "visitors", on how to build battleships and things like that, and use this to conquer white nations. Well, nothing could be worse than this! These are the most treacherous, you know, manipulative, nasty people in the whole world!

In 1915, Sessue Hayakawa, the great Japanese actor, starred in a silent movie called *The Cheat*, which was a big hit. It started a whole trend in Hollywood. In *The Cheat*, he is a suave, well dressed Asian gentleman integrating into white upper class society in america, unlike the crude loud overdrinking white men. He sips tea, he's very soft, he's considerate, he listens to what women have to say … he has this soft manipulative seductive technique. He uses this to get a wealthy white woman into trouble by getting her to overspend on her finances with parties and dresses to the point where she's facing bankruptcy which is of course worse than death because then she won't be up there among the rich. So then of course he opens it up, the package. He will financially rescue her, but she has to become his sex slave, of course. She doesn't have any choice. i mean, if she wants to stay in the upper class, that is. She has to go along and yield herself to this seductive manipulative oriental man.

So white audiences could get the vicarious pleasure of the perversity of interracial sex while seeing how really evil these attractive guys are. But of course, at the last minute she can't go through with it in the bedroom—"No no, I can't do it!"—enraged he tries to force her and then she grabs the revolver which is conveniently left there beside the bed and she shoots him. At which point of course the police and the ministers and all the good white men come in and save her and one of these is a young unmarried white man who falls in love with her and he has lots of money and they live happily ever after.

This turned out to be so popular that Hayakawa made approximately 90 of these silent films. But halfway through he got tired of, you know, "I get killed at the end in every movie. Okay, I know I can't always get the woman, or whatever, but…" By the way, he was the quarterback at the University of Chicago football squad. That's, you know, how he originally got seen by Hollywood. He was in this country and also acting on the sidelines. So Hayakawa said, "No, I can't take this anymore." He started his own production company. In his movies he still doesn't get the woman, and he's still seductively evil and sly, but he doesn't get shot in the end. That's the big thing. And his career lasted until this Hollywood studio said, "Well, you've done well on your own, but we are putting together a big package and we want you to be in it. It's a movie and we call it *The Sheik*. Same plot, but only, you'll be a mysterious … blah, blah, blah." And he said, "No, I'm just tired of this stuff. I'm not going to do it." So they picked this rising actor to replace him, Rudolph Valentino, which was the start of his great career, and the end of Hayakawa's career, not that he was ... he went to Europe, got the hell out of there, out of america, he'd had enough, and settled in France ...

All this time, of course, while all this is going on in people's cultural imaginations, guess what? We're still blue-collar workers. We're still laying railroad tracks. You know, we're picking vegetables on farms. We're just doing what laborers do. 80% of our population was rural at that point in the united states, and many of the rest of us worked in factories. We weren't going to any fancy dinner parties. We weren't seducing anybody. We had no ruling class schemes. We were way down there.

But it was when World War II started, of course, that the Hollywood extravaganza reached its maximum.

There's a Hollywood movie called *Little Tokyo* which was meant to facilitate our removal, in which a white homicide detective goes to investigate a crime and discovers it's part of a series of serial killings. The serial killings, he then discovers, lead into the Japanese-american neighborhood of Little Tokyo and they're done by a Japanese conspiracy. So he goes to Little Tokyo to investigate the conspiracy whereupon the Japanese, using their superior powers of manipulation, manage to convince the rest of the white racist police force that *he* is in fact the serial killer. So our white hero is thrown into prison and put on trial for murder—i mean, how bad could this be? Well, he can't take this. He's got to save law and order and justice. He breaks out of prison all illegally that night and goes to Little Tokyo where he breaks into a meeting of the conspirators, and he discovers that it's not a conspiracy, it's not a little cabal. It's the entire Japanese-american community, thousands of us, scheming together. We're all in it and we're working for Imperial Japan, the Emperor's giving us orders inside fortune cookies or something. The serial killings, it's all part of this plot thing. Well, he eventually of course triumphs, and we're all being arrested by the zillions. He gets a big medal and a promotion, and everybody's happy. Everybody white.

Public expectations about a final showdown race war across the Pacific between white America and "yellow" Japan were widespread way before Pearl Harbor. A colorful example was *Click* magazine, one of the popular pulp fiction monthlies then, which ran a cover story titled "Japs Invade California," predicting concentration camps. Only in their version it's reversed, it's the "Concentration Center for Women, San Francisco" behind barbed wire in their cover illustration and story. And a Japanese soldier holding a rifle and bayonet leers at a line of terrified white women he now has evil power over. So it was only fair for them to do it to us, was the moral of the story, since everyone knew it was only what we'd do or even worse if we could.

Then, of course, the government itself was producing movies like *My Japan* which i can pretty much guarantee nobody here has seen. It was a propaganda film produced by the War Finance Division, a division of the united states Office of War Information; ostensibly to help sell war bonds, but really it's just a race-hate propaganda piece. It opens with this idyllic scene of a Japanese garden; a geisha in a kimono fades into the background, the lily pads in the pond kind of stir in the wind, and the narrator says, "Yes, this is beautiful, but you know, underneath this there's a whole other reality, blah, blah, blah." Then the film goes on to show what this "other reality" is, there's a soldier bayonetting a baby, another shooting prisoners in the head, etc. The same narrator, his voice now with a heavier Japanese accent, bragging about all this stuff. The whole movie is about how Japanese as a race are monsters, who are capable and who want to do anything evil and must all be killed or wiped out.

DURING ALL THIS TIME, we've been kind of having a house moving party ourselves, courtesy of the u.s. Army. Which rounded up all 127,000 of us on the west coast and put us into concentration camps. My father's part in the Imperial Japan conspiracy was working in a fish cannery in Los Angeles. My mom who was the crazy dreamer in the family was a poet. She loved poetry and her family had respected her abilities so much that they let her stay in school long enough to actually get a master's degree from UCLA in literature. Her dream was some day to teach literature in the high schools. My father's was to be an art teacher. They couldn't do that then of course, because we could be the janitor or we could be the school clerk or we could be the woman dishing out the mashed potatoes in the cafeteria, but we couldn't actually be the teacher. That wasn't allowed. Because, you know, us, the Japanese with our evil manipulative ways ... who knows what degeneracy we could bring those poor children into? It's kind of as if we were all gay or something.

So even though we don't have any resemblance to the Imperial Japanese navy, army or anything like that, we're in a concentration camp. That's a whole other discussion in itself, probably two or three, i'm not going to go into that. i want to talk about what happened after the concentration camps.

The odd thing is that right after World War II, the united states occupied Japan, as we all well know, and although they had planned to occupy China, and had actually sent troops to China to occupy it, they got kicked out. A beachhead force of ten thousand u.s. Marines landed in a coastal city—but was forced to leave in a hurry or get wiped out. Bingo! Suddenly there was Communist China which was now the world's worst enemy in Asia, and Japan was now america's best buddy in Asia. Japanese were now good.

Hold it—so that was a little bit confusing. But yes, overnight Japanese were declared "good".

So in 1945, suddenly we were told, "You should start a new life for yourselves because we love you and you should get an education, become middle-class professionals, no telling how far you could go in america. Go for it!" And this label, we hated it, it was given to us: We were the "model minority". Starting after 1945 our whole community convulsively changed. We went for education, went for professional careers, became scattered in middle-class communities in the suburbs, very different.

Completely faked me out, for one. i mean, after the war my father and uncles and their friends used to sit on the back porch after work in the summer. Telling jokes and laughing and dissing each other, just hanging out. i thought they were really beautiful, all tanned in white t-shirts and khakis or jeans with their cigarette packs rolled up in their shirt sleeves. Wanted to be just like that when i grew up. But when i did, when i, too, went in my turn to work at the assembly plants and railroad yards—no Japs! We'd all gone. Like one uncle worked as a tv repairman, but after a night school degree ended up as an engineer in the California aviation industry. And so on like that. There was an auto mechanic here and a cook there, but really us Japs had left blue collar heaven behind us. Left no forwarding address. A whole Asian working-class subculture was wiped out, it seemed overnight to me.

But during those 20 years in the 1950s and 1960s while we were succeeding and living out the american dream or nightmare there was an incidental fact which is that of all ethnic groups including various white peoples in the united states, Japanese-americans had the highest rate of heroin addiction. No, not New Afrikan people, not white poor workers, not hipsters—Japs. For anybody who was around drug clinics back then, which i was, that's an ordinary fact. Well hold it, if we're so successful and things are going so well, why are we shooting up? The rate of alcoholism is even more staggering. My own family was going for the congressional medal of honor there. Why are we shooting up and drinking ourselves to death, at the same time "it's never been better" for us?

The fact is that while they were uplifting us they were also destroying us. This is not approved history. Japanese-american organizations are not going to say these things. But that's what i thought when i was a kid. Because what happened is in five years we had gone through this convulsive shock. We had been primarily rural farm workers and small farmers, then suddenly we were all concentration camp inmates, and then we were supposed to become urban would-be professionals bound for higher education. This was really dizzying. And we were dizzy.

To start with, the whole question of the camps is really funny. These camps were not like ordinary concentration camps. One of the reasons is that after about a year, a year and a half, they lost interest in us. i mean, you know, they put you in a concentration camp, at least they're supposed to be interested in you. But they totally lost interest. We were like someone at the prom abandoned by their date. They stopped guarding the perimeter—like this is serious. In our concentration camp, in all of them, there's that area by the barbed wire outer fence that's completely bare down to the ground. There's supposed to be nothing in that, no rocks, no bushes—nothing—no buildings, no pieces of wood, because that's the kill zone. That's the zone that demarcates how far you have to stay away from the barbed wire, the outer fence. You step into that zone, the guards have orders to shoot you. They don't yell at you, they don't talk to you, they shoot you. In fact, in some of my earliest childhood pictures i'm dressed in what looks like a little boy's brown u.s. army uniform. My grandmother who ran the family was so scared that i would run in, playing, into the zone and get shot that she took one of the precious army wool blankets that we had and cut it up and made a little army uniform for me. "So that the soldiers will see that and they won't want to shoot you," she told me.

But actually, about a year or so later, they didn't care. You could and people did completely open up the barbed wire. You know, people wanted to go out to the well out there and this was inconvenient, so i'm just going to basically cut the barbed wire in this section so that we can just duck under and go—and they didn't care. Then they started saying, "Look, aren't you Japanese bored? Don't you want to go work in the war industry? You can go work in the war industry or work on a farm out here. You can be farm laborers. You can't go west back to California, but you can go east. Go anywhere east and get a job in the war industry."

People were obviously really suspicious, like, "Oh yeah, first you round us up and put us behind barbed wire, then you say 'Oh, just make a run for it.' Yeah, we don't believe that stuff." But finally people started trying it and it seemed to work, so camps gradually started emptying out. So, like, what the hell is this? Oddly enough while there have been many many books written on the concentration camps, nobody has looked at this one thing.

And by the way, the camps themselves were really odd in terms of who got to go there. You see most of the Japanese-american population, 2 to 1 or something like that, were in Hawaii, where we were 40% of the labor force who worked in the war industries at Pearl Harbor on the base. So when someone official said "Let's take all the Japanese in Hawaii and put them in concentration camps," the Chamber of Commerce, the Honolulu mayor, the military governor of Hawaii, the admiral in charge of the Pacific Fleet, they all said, "What? Are you crazy? Like, you know, knock that off! We need these guys!" So that didn't work. And if you weren't in the western military defense zone, i.e. the west coast, you didn't have to go to any concentration camp. If you were

a dangerous, stab-in-the-back, sly, racially untrustworthy Jap in like Milwaukee ... my stepmom grew
up near Milwaukee, she was never anywhere close to
having to go to camp ... New York, Washington, d.c.,
in none of these places did you have to go.

So what's so magical about California? Well the
answer is that we were farmers and we weren't like
white farmers. They had their culture and we had
ours. We had very small farms—average 42 acres
which for u.s. commercial farms is like no farm at
all—using intensive hand labor *à la* Asian agriculture,
much more common in Asia than here—and it turned
out that doing that we accounted for 48% of all fruits
and vegetables produced and sold in California. In
other words, we were beginning to dominate (there
we go again in our sneaky ways) the fruit & vegeta-
ble market in California. The white growers were not
happy. When the war started they saw a wonderful
opportunity, which some of them admitted. "We get
together our politicians like governor Warren, Earl

Warren, and our rich people that are ethnically inter-locked in with us..."—a lot of these farmers were ironically Italian-american and until very recently were supporters of fascism in Italy, but that doesn't bother people—"and we get together with the important friends we have like the Bank of america and push the politicians in California to demand that the Japanese be taken away." Which they did, and it worked very well.

They had a big going away kind of house party for us in which we were allowed to sell or give away every-thing we had. We could take what we could carry. That's all. So if we happened to accidentally have a new car, white people would offer us $50. We had a ranch, a farm—$100, $200 ... or nothing ... some-times, our people just walked off because they were too scared and disgusted with the whole thing. White men would just go to the County Clerk, their cousins sometimes, and say, "Oh yeah, so and so, Mo, the Japanese farmer, he sold me his farm for 50 bucks."

They would just record that in the county records. All legal.

So essentially everything we had was taken from us, in particular our land, our place in agriculture. It wasn't just us of course. There were Japanese-Canadians who farmed in places that would now be called Vancouver. Their farms were lost, no compensation for decades, and even then just a token amount. So essentially white settler america and the ruling class in California had gotten what they wanted from us: Everything we had. Because we had too much for colored people; we shouldn't have that much. And once they'd taken it from us then they didn't care, they were perfectly fine with it if we then left the camps, go east, work in the war industry in Detroit or wherever.

Which my father did—he went to Detroit, got a job in an auto plant making military airplanes. That Saturday or Sunday, whenever it was, the Japanese family he was staying with, they said, "Come on, we'll go to the park, the wonderful park in Detroit by the lake." That was the day that the great Detroit race riot broke out. My father is sitting in the park, eating whatever it is, sandwichs or rice balls or whatever, all of a sudden there's thousands of white men and Black men running all around him, attacking each other with baseball bats and clubs and knives. And that's it—he went home, packed, got on the Greyhound bus—he didn't know what was going on but he was leaving that place. Went to Chicago. Got a job at the old Buick engine plant at 26th and California (a location famous just by its street names here, since that was across the road from the main county jail). And that's how our family ended up in Chicago.

The thing is that when i say we went through what amounts to explosive decompression culturally, this almost can't be overstated. To go through those kinds of changes, what happens to how you think about life ... One of the wonderful features about the official Black history given by the capitalists is there are only heroes. There are no villains, there are only heroes. They're wonderful people, always, the spokespeople, the representatives of the community, etc. Well, i don't know what that might prepare you for, but in our case we had a totally different situation. Our situation is the bad guys won. And i don't just mean white people, i mean the bad guys won. The worst elements in our community won. And that changed things a lot.

So here it is, 1945, end of the war, getting out of the camp, you're starting a new life, what do you do, not as individuals, but as a community? Well, one thing we decided: We're not going to be political. i mean politics isn't exactly going to do us a lot of good was what people decided. Oh, there's radicalism ...

My mom had been with the Communist Party, my father was a social democrat. The social democratic parties had officially passed statements, they opposed the camps, they were for our civil liberties. Which was nice. You know, we appreciated it, but they actually didn't have any power to do anything and they didn't do anything. They were good at that.

The Communists who were essentially 90% of the left at that point from what i can tell, hugely influential, they applauded it. They said, "This is a great idea, take them all to the camps!" My mom was a little surprised you might say. She had joined the Communists because they seemed to be the most militant people fighting racism in California. Now, they're literally applauding as we're being taken to concentration camps. They said, "We don't want to have any distractions like human rights issues, civil rights protests, any internal dissent that would impede the war effort to help the Soviet Union We have to help the Soviet Union! Get the war going, so Japanese-americans can do their part by going to concentration camps!" And they expelled all the Japs in their party, so everyone would get the point. Every good revolutionary Japanese-american should, you know, speed the whole thing along and not fight it but help it, help the authorities put everybody Japanese in prison.

Radicalism you might say was discredited in our community.

Then there was the other faction of political people who meant, i think, well, but they were proponents of Imperial Japan, they were right-wing nationalists. Because america had totally rejected us and democracy didn't work why not support the one place that we could go to—Imperial Japan. So they started Imperial Japanese activities of different kinds in the camps. That was like a big utopian fantasy. They had dreams of what would happen when the Japanese army would free them and conquer Idaho or something. Life wasn't going to work out that way. Nothing against those guys but that wasn't real.

Okay, so militant politics is out. Then the other big problem is there was the faction which was extremely successful. They were the liberal democrats, who were of course pro-u.s. government. Their thing was: "This mass imprisonment is wrong, we all know that, but instead of protesting we want to work with the authorities, to show that we're truly patriotic, that's the only way we'll get established, etc., etc." So they essentially worked closely with the army and the FBI, to have things inside the camps run well. Better known as informers.

Of course i didn't understand any of this, i was just a little kid. But when i was a little older, like seven or eight, in a little playgroup, there was one kid who was really conspicuous because his family was rich. They had a very successful retail business in downtown Chicago which they had gotten—Bing! Just like that! Nobody could figure it out ... right out of the camp they had this business. But the thing is, he's still frankly a Jap kid, he can't play with Nelson Rockefeller's kids, he's gotta play with us. And my father told me, "You can't play with him." I said "Why can't we play with him?" He's a little strange, and he's got all this money, but it's nothing bad. My father explained: "His whole family, they're *Inu*, dogs." i didn't know what that was—i was just a little kid—i knew it wasn't them crawling around on all fours ... maybe that they bit people? i didn't know what he was talking about. Well, the other kids told me, "No, they were informers, and if they had heard you saying something disloyal they would tell the police and you would get dragged away!" Although i didn't know exactly what that would mean.

So these people who were informers, the pro-american helpers of the Army and the administration of the camps, they became our self-appointed political leadership. They had great ties to Washington, to the Democratic Party. They became our representatives and frankly nobody wanted to fight them and people didn't. What people did is they adopted an attitude of, "Your thing"—the pro-government people had their organization called the Japanese American Citizens League—"Fine, your thing will represent us. We won't have anything to do with it but we won't say anything either. You do your thing for yourself and we'll just lead our little lives." 'Cause our community was just stunned culturally and politically. My parents were stunned. They didn't know what to do, other than to get a job, listen to music on records and drink your beer when you come home after work, have dinner, go to bed, live your little life. But as a people we didn't know what to do. And for a while we were stranded in the middle of the Midwest, my family, many of us. What's going on?

i used to complain to my New Afrikan friends, that we didn't even have a green book. This was during the 1960s or the 1970s. One of my friends looked at me and said, "What would you be doing with Colonel Khadafi's, you know, Islamic Green Book?" i said, "No no no no, i mean the *Black* green book." Because back then when i was a kid, New Afrikan people in america couldn't go to most restaurants and hotels and things, so they had their own directory called the green book. A lot of the places that they could go were in the Black community, you know, and were not formally hotels or formally restaurants, but they could stop there to get fed or stay the night. We Japanese-americans didn't even have that because we were just too new, too scattered.

So when we went to the west coast driving, we'd just drive straight through or we'd stop at the side of the road to sleep. If we had to eat we'd go to the market, we'd buy bread and lunch meat because you don't know—half the restaurants are going to refuse you ... some of the others won't let you eat but you can come to the back door like New Afrikans and they'll sell you take-out food ... So, like literally, the ordinary landscape of daily life was confusing to us. We didn't know what we would be allowed to do and what we wouldn't.

Oddly enough, a number of years later, many years later actually, i'm talking to a radical activist, he's active in his local committee to drive McDonald's out of the neighborhood. They want local independently owned restaurants, not the chain fast foods. He needs a wheelchair to get around but he's still active, you know. So we're talking, and i said "Well, got to be honest with you, i mean, McDonald's food is crappy, but i kind of like all these chain restaurants with national headquarters because i know i can use the restroom. i know basically it's safe for me to go there, because as a kid we had those locally owned, locally supplied, locally-white-people-run restaurants that you all want everywhere. Well, we had them already once, you know: They were the people, we didn't know whether we were going to get thrown out, beaten up, insulted … we didn't know what was going to happen. We like these big chains we can lobby, pressure, you know, etc." And he paused and he said, "Well actually, I go to McDonald's all the time because they have the only accessible restroom in the neighborhood." Yeah, so you see my point is that life's not as simple as all that.

My problem then, and i'm just this little kid, is that … what do i do? i mean, we're in the ghetto. Just trying to go to school, have friends … make a life, to be blunt about it. And my community is completely stunned by what's happened. My parents are totally stunned. In fact, they were so stunned that the fact that we were in a concentration camp was like some kind of a secret. Lots of Japanese kids weren't told that until they got into their teen years. i was told by a white man. i didn't know before then.

My parents said "Oh yeah, camp" 'cause they would joke around and sit around with friends and reminisce about "camp". You see when they would say "camp"—they would never say "concentration camp", they would say "camp"—they would tell us later, "Oh yeah, you know we were having fun at camp, like the Boy Scouts do and stuff. That's what we're talking about. You go and play, don't listen to us." So, a lot of us, we had no idea we'd been. That's what it was. So i had to find answers. But i couldn't find them in my own community. i mean they probably existed somewhere in the community but not anywhere that I knew of. My family didn't have answers because when i say that the bad people won, i'm not just talking about politicians. The bad people were winning culturally in our community.

My uncle was one of the first Japanese-american guys in Chicago to become a doctor after the war. The story of how he became a doctor is the story of our transition. He discovered right after he got out of camp that there was a loophole by which he could go to medical school, but he didn't have any money. His father went to everybody he knew in the community—typical immigrant thing—and said, "We want you to invest in my son's education. He could be our first doctor, so we are asking for everybody's life savings, all the money you have ... we'll pool it, send him to medical school, we'll have a doctor and he'll pay you back." So a bunch of families, they gave his father all this money, he went to medical school, became a doctor ... and then my uncle moved straight to the white suburbs, fast as he could, like day one.

By this time, by the time he did his internship and residency, his father had died. So the families who had loaned all this money went to see him out in the suburbs and said, "Well, we're glad that you are a doctor but you kind of left our community and we'd like you to make arrangements to repay the loans." And he said, "What loans?" And he said "You loaned my father money. I didn't borrow any money from you. I don't owe you anything." Showed them the door.

So even though he was a doctor, he couldn't resist ripping off his own people to help start his capitalistic career. He's the guy who was known for being, again, a pioneer: The first Japanese-american in Chicago to face the dilemma of should he buy a European sports car, a Porsche, or a Cadillac. That's what he told everybody in the family. "What should I do?" After he'd ripped off the community, everybody's life savings. And finally he said "I'll buy both!" Because after all he's got all this extra money. It's a miracle to me that he wasn't killed, you know ... frankly, that's why he moved far away out into the suburbs.

So i mean the bad guys were winning in our community. Not just in america.

i knew i didn't want to be like my uncle. And i didn't want to be like Wayne, the rich kid whose family were "dogs" (wasn't quite certain what that all meant, but okay they were bad, you know). But what do i do? i don't want to be like my father who—frankly—he holds a job, he's a responsible dude, comes home, eats dinner, drinks a beer, watches TV, goes to bed. But me ... i mean i'm angry, upset, chaotic, i'm something ... i want to make something different in life. i don't know what. So i had to leave. And we were living in the ghetto, we're going to a New Afrikan elementary school. So i went to the New Afrikan Nation. Just stepped across the line.

Before i had only a little bit of information on the world because Japanese kids' grapevines, our world was little—we only played with each other, other Japanese kids, we only went to other Japanese houses, so we only had this little slice of information about the world—okay, i ended that, crossed that line. Suddenly i'm hanging out with a few Black kids. They have a much bigger gestalt, a much, much bigger vision of the world. It's not my vision, but all of a sudden i'm learning about how they are navigating the world, what that means to them.

One of my friends taught me "the rules". There's some kind of something now called the rules, like about dating or something? Well, when i was that confused child back then, when you said "the rules", you meant the Mississippi rules. Like, how do you deal with white people. How do you act to not be hurt or killed. And the rules were really simple for a colored kid; like, you don't want to talk to a white person ever if you could avoid it. If you have to do it, only say "yes" or "no", don't explain anything, don't give anybody anything, don't go into a long story—say "yes" or say "no" or say nothing. Never look a white man in the face, always look down at your shoes when you talk to him. Never under any circumstances look at a white woman directly. There were all kinds of tactics for how you could be looking at a white woman but appear not to be looking at a white woman, you know.

A lot of the Chicago-born kids, they scoffed at this, they called my friends "country". Because these rules from "seg" Mississippi, they weren't bound by that kind of backward country thinking. But i understood a few years later how Emmett Till got himself into a lot of trouble for allegedly sassing a white woman when he went down South to visit family, and got himself lynched at the age of 14.

i learned white-baiting. i had played Japanese kids' league football and baseball, but white-baiting was actually the first grown-up sport i ever played. The white neighborhood adjoining the ghetto to the south was called by New Afrikan people the "White Highlands" ... and that's kind of after the "white highlands" that the British settled in Kenya. They weren't white just because white people lived there, they were white because unless it was during daylight and you had a job to be there—you were a domestic maid or you were a city garbage collector, truck guy or something—New Afrikan people were not allowed in the area.

So i'm 10 years old, me ... and my friends, right, they're 9, 10, and 11 ... we get on our bicycles and we'd ride into the white community. This is actually a lot of fun for us, you know. And people are astounded, like: "Hold it! What are they doing?" We ride right down the middle of the street, waving "Hi neighbors! How ya doing?" And we're smiling at everybody and within two blocks of course we had a mob chasing us, dozens of white teenagers and men with baseball bats, knives, whatever they have, right? Screaming and cursing at us ... their usual curse, their standard curse thing back then, was "We'll kill you, you little nigger bastards!" And we're laughing like hell because hey, they don't have bicycles, and we're racing like hell. So we've turned around and the game is of course now that you've got the white people stirred up, can you make it to the border? If you can't, you're in a lot of trouble to say the least. But that's the game: Make it to the border! We're going down the alleys, we're cutting through people's backyards...

So this is a whole different world to me—Japanese just weren't doing this stuff—this is like discovering jazz or something, it totally blew my mind! And i started working with the gangs, working for the gangs. (You don't work with the gangs, you work *for* the gangs.) And gradually, piece by piece, i was building a picture of the world that i could use to grow up in.

It isn't true that it was only people of color that i learned from, because i was looking for other people to teach me things that i couldn't find at home too. In high school, secondary school, i ran into or got recruited into a small social clique, basically the intellectuals and outcasts of the school. A lot of them were white kids from left families; their families were socialist or communist. i thought their ideas were completely crackpot—i tell you, i didn't have any politics, but these kids were ... they're 14 years old and they're telling you about how Joseph Stalin is the world's greatest expert on frying pan production! And you say, "You better sit down you know, you're in some fantasy life, man, you know!" Like they were just loyally maintaining the party line that their parents had told them and all that stuff. But while scoffing at them, to admit it, i was also really kind of ... you know, this is during McCarthyism, this is when leftists were losing their jobs, going to prison, being threatened, and here are kids just like me and they're trying to stand up for politics that they know everybody hates them for but they believe in … and you had to kind of admire that.

When i say different angles of perspective, i mean we obviously assume that it isn't just race in that usual official sense of race. My girlfriend during high school came from a lesbian family; her mom was a working woman and her other parent was a butch, Tom, who was an exotic dancer. They had a very tense family to say the least, being doubly illegal, as sex workers and as lesbians, as a family. They were very accepting of me, though, really supportive and actually they were the first family i ever felt at home with, which was really strange.

My girlfriend would hate it when she had to take a note home because there was some problem and there was a parent-teacher conference called. Didn't know all the details because kind of being accepted in the family in that guest-way means that i'm at the outer edge of the life but i'm not in the life, so there's lots that i didn't know. But for some reason i gather there was a thing … maybe a cop thing? That working women in the upper end of the trade who were in effect known and registered with the vice squad—like Mary worked the hotel bars and downtown lounges—they weren't supposed to wear civilian clothing. They weren't supposed to hide who they were? i dunno. Anyway, when Mary came to school for a parent-teacher conference, she'd come in her working clothes and she'd walk in the front door of the high school and everything would stop. Everybody would stop because she is obviously a prossy … and people would stare and she would be walking with tremendous dignity, armored in her determination to have self-respect for herself and for her kid. A lot of courage, more than i've ever had in life, i'd say.

So as a lost kid i had to go outside, searching, and i did find a lot of other peoples of different kinds to learn from, which i really needed. And when the Sixties came, that kind of sharing experience got booted up

on a political level. People would call it "internation-
alism", but a lot of what it really was, particularly for
Asians in a lot of places where we could, we banded
together. Asian-american students at Berkeley and
most of the University of California system forced
a development of Asian-american studies programs.
Berkeley was unique and different because they
demanded that it not be an "academic" program,
that it primarily serve the community and integrate
with the community, and the community would be in
the program and in the building and stuff. (Of course,
as soon as they could the University liquidated all
that, and took it all back to academia...)

But all of a sudden Japanese and Filipinos and Indians
and Chinese and so forth were working together in
the Asian movement on the west coast and the east
coast. And others of us, like Richard and Yuri, were
going into the Black Revolution, an enormous jump.
Yuri Kochiyama ... if you read the *Life* magazine issue
on the death of Malcolm, you'll see one of the final

pictures is Malcolm dead or dying cradled in the lap of an Asian woman, Yuri Kochiyama, who was one of his friends who was there that night he was assassinated. She moved to Harlem, moved by the Black Revolution, and gradually got active and essentially became a major activist there. Not just the ordinary New Afrikan community work but revolutionary nationalist politics, became a registered citizen of the Republic of New Afrika, did armed struggle prisoner support and stuff.

Richard Aoki, in Berkeley, as people who follows scandals know, became one of the earliest members of the Black Panther Party. He was friends at school with Huey Newton and Bobby Seale and he was the first captain and then the first field marshal of the Black Panther Party ... he left to start the Asian American Political Association (or AAPA) which was the first Asian armed self-defense group against the police. It got repressed out of existence but was i would say a noble try anyway ... (Still proud that i have the original yellow AAPA button which Richard gave me ...)

THE THING IS THAT IT'S HARD TO UNDERSTAND NOT JUST THE ROAD THAT WE TOOK PER SE, but also the way race has been used in relationship to us, just from an official paradigm. But that doesn't mean there's no connection. i'm going to go back to the question of the camps, to close.

In 1988, President Reagan signed a bill apologizing to us for being "relocated", as they say—i.e. put into camps—and promising an apology and money for each of us who had actually been in the camps and lived long enough to get that. They delayed and delayed and they were hoping that like only 50 or 60,000 of us would have survived, but actually 80,000 survived; unpleasant surprise for them.

So this was a complete shock to me and i can tell you to a lot of people. There's an official mythology that the Japanese-american left uses and now the pro-government liberals use, that our community fought and fought for reparations till the movement got so big that Washington couldn't resist anymore and they crumbled and that's how we got reparations. That's a total fantasy world. i mean does anybody remember the 500 students storming the White House and the televised sit-in for reparations? No? Because it never happened. How about the 50,000 people, the Japanese-americans who marched on Congress demanding reparations? Oh, you can't remember that? That didn't happen either. The whole thing is imaginary, more "progressive" made-up bullshit. There were small committees here and there, sometimes almost solitary activists with petitions, nothing anything like big because almost no one thought anything was ever going to happen ... in our lifetime anyway. These were good people fighting the good fight to near total indifference.

It was really stunning then that we won the lottery and i sure didn't understand it. i just thought it was another of these weird government things that happen, like surprise income tax refunds or something. i'm just glad it was working in our favor this time. But then the trouble began. i got a phone call from a friend, an Asian activist on the east coast, and she said "Did you know they're setting up these commissions that have hearings all over the country where those of us who were in the camps can go and testify as to what happened and what we think and what we want?" i said, "Well that's good. i've heard that." She said: "So i think you should come to the east coast and testify." That surprised me. i said, "Uh, hold it. Like, i'm not in your group, that party you're with, you got lots of people, so why can't you guys do that? Like, what's stopping you from testifying?" Heard some "Well uh, uh, uh..." More *umm*ing and *ahh*ing ... Okay, finally it comes out: "They made a deal."

You know, sometimes you get these moments in life where what you hear, what you learn is so stunning to you it doesn't get processed? This is one of these moments. i'm thinking: Japanese-american Marxist-Leninists made a deal? Well, who would make a deal with us? What could that be about?

They had literally made a deal. They went to Norman Mineta, Congressman Norman Mineta, who was known as the main sponsor of the reparations bill, although as a loyal "vanilla wafer" he opposed reparations for fifteen years before that. Totally opposed reparations. Not a single one of the Japanese-americans elected to Congress to represent white middle-class people ever supported reparations for us until they got orders to turn about. Although Norman Mineta every year introduced a bill in Congress to make country folk dance the official dance of America. For that he's honored by the country folk dance enthusiasts and associations as kind of their patron saint. Which is good, i'm glad he did something for someone during all those years he was kissing [censored], but he clearly didn't give a damn about us! He's the sponsor of the bill, and they went to him and they made a deal.

i'm thinking fast but in circles—What's this deal? What could it be!? You're going to read Stalin to them or something? My friend said: "The deal is that we're not going to talk about the things they don't want us to talk about. That's unimportant. The important thing is we can talk about socialism and communism." i said, "What? What does that mean?"

i had to wait till i could get someone actually in person so i could browbeat them to tell me what the hell is going on. What's going on is they did make a deal, they made a deal with the government: Their people would testify at the commission and they could say anything they wanted about socialism and communism. They could condemn capitalism in general, in the abstract, all they wanted. There's only two things they agreed not to discuss. i said, "What's secret? What could be secret about the camps that you can't discuss?"

The things we couldn't say was, one: The public hearings are rigged. Turns out you can't testify unless you submit a full text of your testimony in advance, which the committee, the u.s. government bureaucrats, go over and they make sure that it's all what they like. Anything they don't like is stricken. You don't agree with that, you're out, you can't testify. So what my friend was actually wanting me to do is put in a fake testimony and then when it's my turn to come with the mic—scream and shout and protest and they'll drag me out, it will be like one of my old civil rights things. "You did that a thousand times, I mean you know how to do that." So i said well okay, the committee's hearings are rigged, all the testimony is censored, the stuff the government doesn't want public isn't there—okay what's the stuff the government doesn't want public, then? Well, they said, "It's the reparations for the Indigenous slaves." i said "What?! We aren't Indigenous slaves! What are you talking about?"

Well, see, it turns out that it's not about us. That's why we got these reparations out of the blue like a big surprise. This is like the Hollywood movies about the Japanese seducer, only we're now the good guys. We're the cover story. And we're being told, "We'll give you $20,000 each, lots of publicity, lots of apologies, we'll be so sorry. All you have to do is go along and follow our script."

It turns out that the legislation didn't begin with Norman Mineta who always opposed it. It began in 1979 with a white congressman in Washington state. It was about the Indigenous Aleut peoples who were taken at gunpoint from their homes in the Pribilof Islands in the Bering Sea and dumped in the Alaskan winter in old cannery sheds, empty factory buildings with no windows or doors, and basically left to die during the war. Those 800 people suffered losses of about one third of their people. Their lands are to this day ... well, the legalities are kind of you know a little in dispute ... It started about them getting compensation. You see, we weren't alone in being rounded up by the Army and relocated. Under the exact same presidential order that authorized our removal, the Aleut people on the Pribilof Islands were forcibly removed and imprisoned. News to me, for sure. i was like, "Wait, hold it, where does this stuff about slaves come from? What was this all about?" i was kind of freaked out. Well this is what i learned, roughly, since i'm not any kind of historian about this:

The Pribilof Islands are a few islands southwest of Alaska in the Bering Sea leading to Siberia. It's where 80% of the fur seals go to. When the Russian tsar, in the middle of the 19th century, when his explorers took those islands they made some of the Aleut people move from Siberia to be a serf labor force for their fur trade for which they made a lot of money. They killed thousands of Indigenous people in the process of course, but we all know that's "progress". In 1867 they sold all of Alaska to the united states—"Seward's Folly" it was called. One of the major reasons the united states bought Alaska was they wanted the fur trade, but the fur trade was actually dependent on a slave labor force of Indigenous people.

So the same rules that governed their life under the tsar simply continued under the united states and eventually under the Fishery Department and the Department of Agriculture. The rules were really simple back then. The Aleut people on these islands are allowed to work in the fur trade for the u.s. government. They're not allowed to have any other job. They're not allowed to leave the islands. They're not allowed to communicate in any way with anybody outside the island, the island they're in, without permission of the u.s. government overseers. i mean you have captive workers, you don't want people to know about it obviously. So you're incommunicado.

You don't have to work for them—you could die of starvation. Okay by them.

Year after year, until the 1960s, these people were slaves. Finally, in the 1960s a local politician, a white politician in Alaska running for the state assembly, said "You know this election is really close. If I could get a few hundred of those Indian votes out there from the Aleutians, why that might be the difference!" So he called up to make the arrangements and they said "No." He said, "What you mean no? I'm running for office and I want to talk." They said, "First of all, you're not allowed to come because there's no visitors to our islands that we don't approve of and we don't need a politician on our islands riling up the Aleuts. Secondly, they're not your constituents because they are primitive people they're not really americans. Thirdly, they can't vote for you because they don't have the right to vote. We've never given them that. So goodbye politician."

He was like a little flipped out, so he started introducing bills that maybe they should have the right to vote. Eventually a series of bills during the 1960s freed the Pribilof Aleuts from in effect a legalized form of u.s. government slavery. This is the 1960s, 100 years after the u.s. Civil War. This is what we're not supposed to say. That's why there's a million articles about Japanese-american reparations back then, about the legislation, and the this and the that, but it's all about us. We're the success story. Them, few or no mentions. Because they don't want to admit what they did.

But it's actually more than that. Buried in the bill that gave us money—they're not going to give us money for nothing, everybody knows that—there's clauses. They say roughly this: The money is still being negotiated out. We're not sure how much every person will get because we don't know how many people/survivors there are, we do not know how much the total pool of money is yet, so that will have to be settled later but whatever is decided, the Aleut people must get *less* than the Japanese-americans. They cannot get the *same*. They must get *less*, because while the Japanese-american removal was unjust, it must be clear that the Aleut ethnic removal was *just*, was good and legal.

This isn't just because they're trying to hide something or justify something bad that they did in the past. This isn't about the past to the capitalist state. They're talking about the *future*.

It turns out that eventually i got a letter with the cheque from Bill Clinton, William Jefferson Clinton, on fancy White House stationary: *"Sorry ... blah blah blah"* ... it had all those famous words, "we promise it will never happen again." Foolish me, i thought that meant no more concentration camps by the u.s. No, that's not what it means. It means we promise that we'll never take you loyal Japanese-americans away from California and put you in concentration camps, not that we ever keep our promises in any case, but that's all that we're promising.

The position of the u.s. government is: Why was the Aleut removal from their slave conditions to be dumped into near genocidal confinement in Alaska during the war, why is this just? It's just because the military had a better need, a better rationale for doing it than in the other case for taking Japanese-americans from Los Angeles. And there's two layers to the cake. The first layer is whether it was the right tactical or administrative decision. The Supreme Court has ruled it wasn't but only in our case. In terms of us, they were loyal so you didn't need to take the Japanese-americans and put them into camps. Sorry they lost all their agricultural ... their farms and businesses and homes and everything else ... but you didn't need to take them for that reason. The second thing is what's important: Does the government, does the state have the *right* to do ethnic targeting, ethnic removal, ethnic cleansing? The legal american answer is yes, it does. That's what this is all about.

What's really important here about Japs is not the rights. They're doing all the reparations shit—"We're so sorry, it's racist injustice, blah blah"—but it wasn't racist injustice, it was imperialism. They aren't sorry one fucking bit and i can tell that because guess what: They don't want to give up their *right* to do it again, to give up a single bullet in their arsenal. Their position is if they see a need for whatever the state's interests are—to remove an entire people, to imprison an entire people, to do whatever they want to an entire people—they the state have that overriding right. We don't have any rights, the state has all the rights it turns out. That's why the u.s. empire is posing so hard as the No. 1 champion of human rights around the world. To cover up what they are planning to do next.

A former law school teaching colleague of President Obama's, federal judge Richard Posner, who's generally considered the leading, most important conservative legal theorist in the united states, he flatly says—the Korematsu decision, the key legal decision that the concentration camps were okay— he says, *"correctly decided,"* no doubt about it. Too bad for those people, but correct decision. The former, i can barely remember his name, William whatever it is—Rehnquist, the Chief Justice of the Supreme Court who retired and died a while ago—in his last book, he said flat out front: If there's another situation where the u.s. government wants to do this ethnic concentration camp shit, the future Supreme Court will *"no doubt"* approve it. Well hold it. So what they're saying is if they want to remove Arabs or Asian Muslims, if they want to put them into concentration camps or shunt poor Black people into Sowetos, whoever they think is a problem, even though most of the people are innocent of anything, they could do racial anything-they-want. Because they have that legal power and there's no indication so far that anyone is taking this power away.

They don't want to have that discussion. They don't want to discuss the fact that they want to retain the power, the *right* to do ethnic targeting, ethnic removal, ethnic cleansing. All the apologies and all the memorials and all the reparations for us were just good cover-up for the racist crimes they are going to commit next. Cheap at the price, too.

When do we expect that racism will be ended in america? i would say that racism is going to be modernized. Racism will evolve. Racism is going to have a lot more cover. i don't think racism is ever going to be ended in the slightest until capitalism ends and is buried.

Thank you for listening.

QUESTIONS & ANSWERS

Q: *There's two things i wanted to ask. One is, the term "unimportant minority", why are you using that term? If can you break that down a little bit? My understanding of it, like you gave the example of the fisherman at the beginning, it seems to me like you're saying that Japanese-americans at a certain point in time are that "unimportant minority" and u.s. race relations is white/Black, and those unimportant minorities either become—you didn't use that term but I'm going to use the term—traitors to what they're supposed to be in terms of the "model minority", and join with oppressed peoples, in your context it was poor Blacks in Chicago, and be that, and be a traitor to what your community wants you to be. I just want you to break that down, because I didn't understand all of it. What do you mean by an "unimportant minority"? You said* at the beginning this is very specific to your context, Japanese-americans. But do speculate as to who these other unimportant minorities are, historically or even now. Because it's useful, in terms of some of the other discussions I'm hoping to have with other folks about this.

The second point, I'm not sure if it's a question. I couldn't help but think for the entire time that you were giving your presentation about the context in this settler state of what is called Canada. Over the past few years there have been apologies for the Chinese Exclusion Act, for the Komagata Maru which was a shipload of mainly Punjabis who came over, there was the centenary of that recently, for Native residential schools. For example with the Komagata Maru one there was a statement put out that I'm now regretting signing, I may actually retract my signature, and you know it said "stamps and apologies are a small step towards reconciliation"—and I'm like, no they're not and why do you even want to reconcile with this? Different ways, *subtle ways, that different minorities who have been aggrieved are meant to fit in through these apologies which so many members of our communities, whether it is the Punjabi community or the Chinese community, have been fighting for, for years. Again, I'm not sure if that's a question, I am just making the parallel with this settler state. So let's leave it at that, and just see what you have to say.*

A: As usual, Jaggi, you have asked so much i'm not certain how to answer it all! Though i appreciate the fact that your questions are like mini-briefings all in themselves, reminding us about things we shouldn't forget.

There's a problem. One of the questions you're kind of asking me, to cut to the chase, is: How is it, what do I think about, being a crazy outcast who most people in my community think you absolutely shouldn't listen to or you won't be middle-class enough. This is a hard thing to deal with for almost everybody, because we find ourselves breaking with our families. We definitely find ourselves breaking with our communities over issues. We also need to find those positive roots to grow on.

Like, after 9/11, when the cry arose for ethnic screening and police surveillance over all Arabs and Muslims in general, the Japanese-american community was the only one outside those targeted to protest, to speak almost universally against the onrush of the so-called anti-terrorist measures. Obviously, because we ourselves had been down that same road. Star Trek's "Lt. Sulu", the actor George Takei, bitingly asked reporters, "After the Oklahoma City bombing, did we go around killing white American males?" A deeper question than it might appear on the surface.

So what is an unimportant minority? Ever since i started using that phrase, half the people who hear it come up and ask me what it means? Which is interesting. The literal meaning of the two words are not obscure, but the simple phrase seems ... confusing, or somehow not in any framework of relevancy to people? Or it isn't what anyone is supposed to say? i use it to play with the culturally enforced capitalist lie that all races are "equal" and all races are important. This is their slickly polished veneer of neo-colonial puffery that keeps our attention obediently off the realities of race. Like what it means for some of our peoples for late capitalism to decide to admit us into their social structure as "assistant white men, second class"? As if you can be an "equal" by having a role making the meals or repairing the plumbing in someone else's house. And, obviously, to really be an important "other" to the self-appointed master race of imperialism, you have to be understood as an actual threat to their whole lives. Otherwise, none of us are really any more important to them than Lassie was. Maybe less. i mean, let's grow up here.

The two things that i'm trying to stress is that all of us have to find our own—not somebody else's—angle of experience and vision to let us make our contribution as a people. As individuals, yes, but as peoples also. i mean, my people's history even though i'm hardly representative of them is a source of a lot of things i understand, and there's always been a lot of teaching going back and forth between different peoples for me. i learned from kids, 'cause this terrible need for learning started for me when i was a kid, and I taught other kids, too, back and forth. And i came at an odd time—a lucky time—it was the end of the 40s and the early 50s when oddly enough the Japanese were very popular in the New Afrikan community.

So much of the real world isn't written in the capitalist books. That's one of the nice things about reality, we always have surprises. The rulers think they know all this shit but they don't. Richard Aoki and i once spent an afternoon—this was way long after his Black Panther phase, though he still would spend nights sometimes sipping some and talking old times with Huey—discussing how certain Japanese cultural traits helped us in other people's communities.

The thing that i didn't know as a kid, is that Black servicemen, GIs coming back from their military service … they had served in Asia, so they were in Japan. They came back and they were telling their kids and their friends that Japan is this really fantastic country. Why? Because we're not treated like dirt there. You know, we're just treated like ordinary people and hey, they have different food, different customs, different this and that … you know, it's just interesting to be there. There's a lot of pro-Japanese just ordinary-people-feelings in the Black community at that time and it led to a lot of different stuff to be sure.

My kiddo friends taught me a lot but then they were also peppering me with questions in return, too; it wasn't a one-way street. From their point of view, they wanted to know all this stuff i'm almost embarrassed to talk about it's so childish. But we were kids, we were like nine years old or something and they had real questions. Kids, they don't think the same ways that adults do, right? So they had these burning questions: Was it the u.s.-Japan peace treaty? Was it the issue of the american bases there? No. Their questions were like, "We hear all our uncles and fathers coming back telling us Japanese women really like Black men cause Japanese men have such small penises. Is that true?" Well you know, i'm standing naked in the shower in gym where little kids have these conversations, not hiding the equipment, and i say "Uh, it might be true ... um, i don't know ..." This is not a topic i knew a lot about, i didn't know a lot about sex at that point. "It might be true. Okay, maybe it's true. i don't know." So they were real "Right on!"—they were really happy about that possibility! Okay, so they said, "We also hear that Japanese women are so different that their slits aren't up-and-down, they're horizontal. Is that true?" And i said "Hold it dudes—i got three sisters and can tell you that's not true—forget that!"

The third question they really really had to have answered was ... back then if a teacher caught you or heard you saying a dirty word you were punished, so they had developed this word that they used. Blah blah blah, whatever it was. They said it to each other so nobody else would know what they meant, and they decided that this word meant "go fuck your mother" in Japanese. So that's the big swear word they used back and forth with each other in class and the teachers didn't know what they were saying so they were really happy—and they just wanted me to confirm that's really what it meant. i told them, "Guys, i've never heard that, in life. i highly doubt that's true, but you know, maybe, who knows?"

Well, obviously what happened is some New Afrikan kid got that brainstorm, some kiddy genius got that brainstorm in third grade or something and invented this whole idea of their own words. By which they could invent new curse words that the white teachers didn't know and they could use them. Kiddy genius!

And then older students taught them to younger students and it became an institution in the school. Probably didn't exist anywhere else. And i never heard that word before and i'm pretty sure that it had nothing to do with Japanese but we had that kind of kiddo conversation, not yet adult conversations. But it was political, too, and they shifted my world a little degree on its axis towards the coming light.

It was a lot easier to really be together as kids than it is as adults. Part of the reason is that we all just have a long way to go, we grownups. Example: i was temporarily with Oakland CORE (Congress of Racial Equality) in the early 60s for a little while, doing pickets and boycotts of white stores in the Bay Area that wouldn't hire Black people at all. There were a lot of them. This is San Francisco and Oakland and Berkeley i'm talking about. The Japanese-american families driving out of the parking lot passing our picket line would stop and we'd talk and usually they'd say something like: "I admire you people. This is really good. But you know, are you sure you should be doing this? 'Cause you know you could get in trouble with the law." Some Japanese-americans said to me—because that's the way we thought after being concentration camped, not now, not necessarily people now—they said, *"Are you sure this is the right thing for us? It's right for Black people, but you know white people always have to be attacking someone, and if they're not attacking Black people aren't they just going to attack us again?"*

This was a sincere question and in fact a couple of my aunts had put the same question to me. i said, "No, because if we keep kicking them in the ass all the time they won't be attacking anybody soon. But the other thing is we can't keep thinking that way." But when i tried to talk to comrades, some Asian-american revolutionaries, about it, basically it kind of got tossed out of the room, out of the discussion ... people were yelling at me, "That's a lie! No Japanese would ever say that!" i'm thinking, "Hold it, that's what

Marxism has taught you? After you read Mao and all this? i'm not arguing it's good or anything, just telling you about a conversation we had with people, about how i think it's important that we have to fight people's confused consciousness about this." And this comrade kept saying, "No, this is a lie. We are totally for ... blah blah blah blah ... our people are progressive!" All this other shit. Well of course if you pretend that, then you're not going to bother educating people, you're not going to be fighting about real life messy politics or what people actually think. It's just going to have that movement middle class clear plastic veneer over things.

Like, there was a Japanese-american guy ironically named "Tom" who was probably ... became the biggest cheese in our tiny community in Chicago. He was the first Japanese-american there to rise into management in the public school system way back when. He became an assistant principal and then shifted to become head of buildings and facilities. Tom even got the Order of the Rising Sun from the Japanese government, as well as other local honors. He was pretty much 100% unimportantly obscure in real life, of course, in the larger u.s. society. Nowhere as important to the ruling class as their waiter at Ralph Lauren's Polo lounge in Manhattan, for instance.

But for a second he got his local moment of fame, although it's since been whited-out of memory like it never happened. In the 1960s a teenage Japanese-american girl joined one of the most militant young Black sit-in organizations. She was doing demonstrations and tenant organizing and all that, a high school kid. Tom reacted instantly as a Japanese-american authority figure and got her permanently expelled from school so other Asian girls wouldn't get rebellious ideas too. He even went so far as to get a court order barring her from ever setting foot on any public school property anywhere in the city. She didn't deserve education since she was challenging white supremacy. That really made his career, since the white power structure saw he was so loyal it was like a minor super power, willing to step on his own young people to protect their decaying color line. He really was "Tom".

Eventually, he died and became even less than he ever was. The oppressed don't forget so easily, though, since our own memories are sometimes the only reality that's ours. Many years later, a Japanese-american man came to the office of that high school. He had a problem. He had never graduated but needed something as close to a diploma as he could have so he could get into night classes at junior college. The women clerks at the office dug out his records and looked through them and one said: "You're her brother aren't you? It was your sister who gave up high school wasn't it?" The man said that yes it was his younger sister. The Black woman filled out some official form and stamped it and gave it to him. "This says that you graduated with your class. We've never forgotten what she did you know."

One problem with the reparations discussion in the Black community is a lot of the people who raised it, raised it using *us* as a fantasy example. "The Japanese people got $20,000 apiece; that's because Japan's so powerful economically that the Japanese corporations forced them to do it! So we should get the African Nations to force them..." These are actually completely fantasy ways of thinking about politics that don't deal with actual classes and actual capitalism.

So everybody has a problem of pandering to the backwardness of their own communities and struggling with that which as we all know in reality is not easy.

You implicitly asked thirty other questions i know, but i can't answer them right now...

Q: *Thanks for your talk. It was really great. I really appreciate at the end how you made the links between capitalism and racism. I'm kind of new to the whole paradigm of looking at things from a people of color perspective, but it's made so much sense to me because as people of color we really face a common enemy. For a long time I felt like and I still kind of feel that a common enemy is white people—no offence white people in the room!—but what your talk showed is that the common enemy is also really capitalism, because capitalism in a lot of ways is like the tool and the motivation of white supremacy. But I feel like even in a non-capitalist system, like whatever that would be, white supremacy could still thrive and be successful because of these different ways, different avenues to get together and maintain control and power...*

And just one other small piece to add to that is just from a numbers perspective. I do some stuff around immigration, and I really feel like a lot of the anti-immigration sentiment or the anti-immigration laws or whatever is really purely just a numbers game, and that for white supremacy to continue to thrive there really has to be like a white majority numerically. Even in a non-capitalist system I feel that you could still pursue those kinds of things, so I'm just wondering how do you fight white supremacy in a non-capitalist system, if that makes sense?

A: These are real kinds of issues, because people are ... you know, it's not a small thing that oppressive societies with ruling classes have created cultures. What is culture, but people? It's the way people live. People have traditions and ways of looking at the world that are essentially pro-oppressor, that see themselves as better than other people, deserving to rule other people, and we see this all over the world. i mean, if you want to look at settler colonialism you could look at Canada, you could look at the united states ... you could also look at China. The Dalai Lama may be a completely reactionary religious figure, the Tibetan people may be totally misled about things, i'm not an expert on that, i don't know about this ... but i'm not a fool. i see that China is essentially Han supremacist. What they call Communism is really Han nationalism. And they intend to expand what they think of as the real people, the Han, their culture, into other areas whether they're wanted or not. Take over, essentially replace a lot of these populations. Pure settlerism. i mean no different than Canada or the united states except that biologically the people look different. But it's still settlerism.

So can all of these inherited cultures, these ways of oppressing people, persist after capitalism? Well we're kind of a long way from being after capitalism so i don't expect anybody to have to use these answers any time soon, unfortunately, but certainly that's possible and people will have to deal with it.

Q. *Or even if we create community among each other in sort of a separatist way ... and in a non-capitalist fashion ...*

A: Absolutely, it's a problem. We don't have a good enough culture, to be really kind of blunt about it. i mean culture isn't a marching band, culture isn't a poetry reading; culture is the way we live and the way we solve problems and the way we either help people or don't help people. i mean, what is our real life, what is that like? We have a long way to go. We don't have to be ashamed of it, it's just a fact. A lot of it is the baggage that we've all inherited and carry around on our backs without ever thinking about it.

Q: *How can we, in a situation where justice is understood in monetary terms, getting a piece of paper saying we're sorry and here's your cheque, but there is no real change—how can we resist that, how can people in communities being offered that cheque, resist that, and say no we want fundamental change?*

A: Malcolm X said people talk about that capitalism and that colonialism and that imperialism, but you know you haven't seen anything till they put that dollarism on you. That's, like, really true. And it isn't just offering us money ...

We force them to make changes, to give something up. They don't want to make them, if it was up to them we'd all be slaves. Every single one of us, if you left it to them. The only reason we're not isn't because they've evolved and they're nicer or more modern people, it's because we've forced changes. They can't do things like they used to. i mean capitalism is one world system. There's tons of slavery today as we all well know, diverse places in the system, actual slavery, so they're in no way abandoning slavery as a form of oppression. So what is going on in that sense?

What it is, is we're forcing them to make changes, to give up leverage here and there. But they try to make the concession in a way that perpetuates and strengthens their power. Like "Okay, we're sorry we took your land, we'll keep the land but we'll give you some money." They do that with Indigenous people all the time, constantly. Because the money will eventually just get recycled back into their system, but the fact that they kept the land—the Black Hills, or wherever that land is—that isn't going to get recycled. They're just going to hold that.

It's not a question, in that sense, to me. This is just part of the struggle. It isn't like there's the struggle and then okay the struggle's over and now they're offering us money as a settlement. That's not the end of the struggle. The struggle is going way beyond that and this isn't like rhetorical on my part, but we had experiences ... once in a militant community struggle where we had a small but eager working-class group. This is the story of a battle i tell a lot when i get a chance because it's the kind of thing that gets covered up, deliberately forgotten.

The raw ability and will of the oppressed to remake the world, brushing the rulers aside for a moment even now.

We had this meeting with the Indigenous comrades in our neighborhood. We had a deal with them where we worked 50-50, but not the usual left movement way of 50-50. Our 50-50 is we picked the project that we wanted to do, they'd support us and we called all the shots. Then they'd pick the project they wanted to do and they called all the shots.

So we had a meeting, and they explained their project: "Problem is, our people, a lot of them are homeless, they're really poor, we meet with the city, we go to the Indian cultural centre, the city representatives come and they say 'Well, we're going to improve welfare, we'll have a social work counselor,' you know, blah blah blah, but actually, you know, in real life there's still going to be a lot of Indigenous people homeless and we all know that. That's just reality."

So the Indigenous group said, "What we propose is there's an empty apartment building. We propose to take it. You can help us. We're taking rifles, shotguns, pistols. We're taking the building. It's waiting for the developers. It's got like 40 something units. It's right on Broadway Avenue, main business street on the North side. We'll take the building. You'll help us. That's 50-50. And then when the police come, we'll shoot them."

This is their story really, completely, not ours. Am going to focus just on two things that they did that proved important, that we can learn from.

We followed them. i can't say that we weren't scared shitless, since we really were. They did it. Empty building, it had padlocks on the doors—they broke through, flooded the building with people, their people. So they had about 75 warriors, with guns, and other people, just ordinary people ... lit candles, lit up the building ... had sleeping bags, moved in! Of course the building was 20 degrees or something, in the middle of the cold weather.

So sure enough the police noticed there's people in the building, they come. "Okay you gotta get out of here or we're going to arrest you all." So Mike the main guy said, "Well actually this is the deal: We're not leaving, so you're going to have to give us everything we need to live in this building." The police said, "No, you don't understand, we're going to come here with a SWAT team and we're going to arrest you and those of you who resist will be killed."

We were a little unhappy, but anyways, Mike said, "No, this is our thing, we'll have a compromise. There's no heat. You get a mechanic in and a fuel oil delivery and turn the furnace on and then you bring food for us and if you don't do it by 5 a.m., we're going to start shooting out this window at every white person we see and basically at not the people, but the cars. All the white commuters going downtown, we're going to be shooting at them starting at 5 o'clock." By the way, they didn't tell us this part when we agreed to this action, they neglected that small part...

So the cops said "You crazy Indians, blah, blah, blah ... You can't get away with this." The usual things that cops say. And then Mike replied, "No, your mayor is running for re-election, so either you do what we say or we're going to have a big gun battle here, lots of people are going to get killed, not just Indians, white people, and you know, is that what the mayor wants? You call up your boss and ask him if that's what he wants or does he want to give us what we want?" Smile. Cop stormed out.

Sure enough, an hour later, white guy in a truck pulls up in the alley. He's the furnace mechanic. They woke him up. He's fixing the furnace, the oil comes, there's food deliveries ... So this is interesting! This tactical approach isn't a universal panacea; a lot of places, a lot of cities, you do that and you're going to get killed.

i mean you won't actually succeed, tactically. Maybe there will be a great symbolic victory, but you won't succeed militarily anyway. But the way they timed it, organized it, the particularities, playing off the mainstream politics in Chicago at the time, they had a whole lot of leverage that nobody realized, and they could use that leverage really well. Took smarts and courage both. Also it made a difference being "crazy Indians", since the pigs really understood that Mike and the young guys with guns meant every bit of what they said.

So what did the police do? And the city? They just waited the armed occupation out. Played nice, did nothing overt. Week after week, month after month, we all held the building. They said okay, fine, we'll negotiate. They made all these promises, they had all these great speeches. But basically they were just waiting the militants out because to be honest, we're too messed up. It's really hard. Nothing's happening day after day, week after week. Nobody risked their lives to get bored day after day. People start drinking. There start to be fights.

Mike, the leader, gets stabbed trying to break up a fight. Then Mike asks people to leave because the hostilities are growing so great that some Indigenous families have to move out because they are feuding with other families. "And incidentally, there were people talking about fighting the other people so you'd best move out too. Because," Mike says, "I don't want you to suffer because of my people's problems." So eventually it all falls apart and the takeover gets abandoned, but from the *inside* because people aren't together enough to hold everything in hand to accomplish these things.

There's not an easy answer. We're talking about justice and injustice and beyond. We're talking about power for oppressed people. We're talking about getting rid of capitalism, pushing it out of people's lives as best we can. So we have to be able to shape struggles so they have a better arc in that sense, and we have to be able to actually have power. Not power in an authoritarian structured sense but in a "people" sense, where ordinary people have power. Because they feed on each other: Powerlessness creates cultures where people fuck up all the time, frankly.

Q: *I wanted to go back to the question about the term "unimportant minority". Why are they unimportant? Are we referring to Asians, East Asians, non-Black people of color in general? Are we unimportant because there are numerically fewer of us in the states or is it because the history of our struggle has been repressed and erased? Or is it because we are model minorities being absorbed into the white structure? And further to that, I've heard a fair amount on the internet about this absorption of at least East Asians, or at least Chinese- and Japanese-americans and -Canadians,*

into whiteness. So we might become white in the near future and cease to have a politic in common with people of color as a critical solidarity construct, and I was wondering if you had any thoughts on that.

A: Well i use the term "unimportant minority" ironically and i use it deliberately because that's what capitalism thinks so i want to put it on the table. To really not avoid and really see and think about it ... Isn't it interesting how we keep coming back to this, to these harmless looking words?

i mean they have a white/Black paradigm because to them that's what's important and they don't feel particularly threatened by most of us. Just like it used to be that if you were Mexican you were completely unimportant to them—hold it! You're not unimportant anymore! Things are changing. It's not a static thing.

It's the way they've constructed things and in that sense it's nice to know what they think and how they are trying to condition us to think. But it's much more important to figure out what we think, what we want to do. And absolutely I believe that people of color who ...

... you don't have to struggle against racism and white supremacy and settler-capitalism if you don't want to. You can always not fight, right? And lots of people choose not to. We have to actually struggle with people to reach that point where they see that they have to put that down and move ahead and join other people and learn from other people and teach other people what we can contribute to. And it can't be a discussion on capitalism's terms, on their ground, how they define us. Because that's actually what the battle is about, whether we're going to be what they define us as or whether we're going to determine who we as peoples are.

It isn't just that capitalism is propagandizing us to death, and we're so slow that we don't catch on. People of color almost have to be sharp here, in this land that's both ours but really not ours, to always think of being in some kind of danger and survival silently being there as a question. These angles of attack by capitalism catch us at our weak point, where we want to feel important ... frankly, more important than other people and we think deserve to get more though its uncouth to say that out loud in public. We, too, go along with some phony racespeak echoing through society's loudspeakers, because it covers our act up and actually everyone's act up. That's our complicity.

Like, it's natural to think right away, maybe Asians are unimportant because there are so few of us comparatively. That's in a small part maybe true, obviously. But not primarily, since our importance and unimportance are determined way deeper than that. i know that Japanese-americans too often want to have it both ways, to be allies of all people of color in public and yet, in the pinch, to be trusted allies of white people. We publicly stand with other people of color when racist outrages occur, as long as it doesn't cost us anything.

But when white people need us to join their united front on issues like the whole right-wing thing of testimania, of SAT scores and other abstract white-invented scores being the only "fair" way to judge who gets into good schools and who doesn't, then we're on their side. Only now its "our" side. Asians as we all know have now eclipsed white people as the largest slice of the U. Cal Berkeley student body, with over 40% of admissions. So many Asian students are blasting the roof off of these SATs and other abstract scoring systems that it's like women's pro golf being the metaphor for life, which it isn't. Elite Ivy league schools like Harvard have had to install a home security system to keep out Asian home invaders—a rigid Asian admission quota to keep our numbers down to merely very large. On the quiet, of course , because you don't advertise your racial home security. White society is putting up with this turning the tables so far, because it "proves" that their biased system of educational testimania is "fair" and that excluding Black youth and Indigenous youth and Latino youth and poor working class youth in general may be racial but not racist. If anyone can believe that illogical formulation with a straight face. So we few Asians, we are more important than we give ourselves credit for.

As long as we're talking about unimportant minorities, we should check out the reality that the euro-settler ruling class is always changing the whole game up on us. There's nothing that we own here, it's only loaned.

i can remember when East Asians were the important minority in terms of tokens of upward mobility and political sideshows. When government agencies liked to hire a garnish of us to make their agencies taste better. When at one point there were several Japanese-americans in the u.s. senate, even a Japanese-american state governor, and three or four Japanese-american representatives in the u.s. house at one time. To represent all twenty-five of us? After a while being so safe meant that we no longer were exotic enough, we'd lost that Charlie Chan flavor. So now South Asians are more preferred by government agencies and euro-settler politics, although white folks aren't ever going to admit it.

Are some people of color going to become white? It isn't just happas we're talking about (in the old days called them zebras), but the whole thing of an advancing edge of middle-class people of color settling into white suburban or urban life and integrating, becoming just another kid or just another housewife with a white life among many. Working in the very wealthy white suburbs, i've seen this but don't pretend to know enough about it to analyze it. Of course, i was just the "hey, boy!" and they were the customers.

i hated it, but a number of our Asian customers deliberately sought me out for service, for whatever reasons. One young Chinese-american woman (not FOB) was really nice. Used to come often with her toddler daughter. She was married to a successful German banker who worked in downtown Chicago. They had maids and all, so she had nothing to do all day except drive around with her daughter, window shopping and browsing and buying lots of things 'cause its rude there to always look but never buy. She bought shit from us every week just to be polite. Drove away in her BMW station wagon and probably threw it all away, she didn't care. Not a culture i would want.

One couple, the wife was white and acted very friendly, although clueless in the usual white way. Kids never spoke. The husband was a Japanese national, a university professor, and he clearly hated us Japanese-americans. Used to spend a half-hour every time pretending to be solicitous while really taunting me. You know, "Oh, so you've worked here so many years but you aren't the owner and you're an American citizen too. So sad. Was it hard being in the concentration camps? It's so sad."

Another customers i can't forget were Korean, who wanted to window shop and look and ask questions and linger and finally maybe buy some cheapest thing possible. The older mother and her teenage daughter. They were so clearly down and depressed i hated to see them coming. Finally, one morning, here they all were in the morning newspaper. The husband had become wealthy by fraud, was in court and losing it all, he was beating them up all the time at home, and yesterday had shot them to death and committed suicide.

So i suppose amidst all that there's also lots of cases of successful "Caucasianality", of Asians grow-ing up in the 'burbs and being so culturally stuffed with whiteness that they think Asian culture is using chopsticks when they eat fake Chinese takeout. Jury is out on that, we'll have to see. In some ways to me it's like them sending the man to the moon—you know, it changed everything but you can't find anything it changed.

Remember, they always want to box us in. To misthink that we can only choose either to go back to our "traditional" ways—which we can't unless someone at Samsung invents a time machine—or give in and adopt modern white culture and roles. Actually, we don't have to do either, and shouldn't. We can take the best from what we brought with us. We can improvise and create new culture and they can stuff their roles. We have the power of the people.

Q: *I had a question not about something you said tonight but about something that you said in an*

interview. You said that what was happening in america right now is that america is being desettlerized. I was just wondering if you could expand on that. If I look at Arizona or New Mexico or some context like that, it seems pretty clear to me. But I'm wondering how you feel that that relates to your context in Chicago, I feel like that may be more similar to the context here, where migrants aren't Indigenous to the land. What's your view of the connection between desettlerization and decolonization?

A: Okay, It's complicated. And it's complicated for two reasons. First of all, we're talking about historical time, historical processes, not talking about the next election in five years or something like that.

Settler colonialism is a specific form of colonialism which we see a lot of here, but there are lots of areas in the world where they don't see it, right? Settler colonialism is where the colonizing nation imports an entire population to be its arms and legs and soldiers and whatnot. Around the world, the original settler colonialism in countries like Algeria, Kenya, and so forth, essentially has largely disappeared. There were a million French Algerians in Algeria and Algeria was a province of France, not a colony, a province. The teaching of Arabic was illegal because French was the only legal language of France. When finally in order to end the guerilla war and get access to the Saharan oil, General de Gaulle had to agree to let the Algerians rule Algeria, a million French settlers left. They felt totally betrayed. They are the basis, in fact, of the French right in the south of France. So it isn't like suddenly they found the light and therefore world revolution or something. To some extent this is starting to happen in North America, at least in the united states. It's not happening rapidly, but in historical terms it's rapid.

i mean the guys i used to work with before getting laid off and the company closing—all the other guys were Mexican, a Mexican crew, i mean native Mexican not

Mexican-american—they had a completely different drift on politics than i did, totally. They understood what i was talking about, though. Their grandfather who was the first one from their *colonia* who got a job in our company, he loves Che Guevara. He's for revolution, you know, he's into this Sixties stuff. The younger guys respect him personally but they think he's politically out of it.

They're for whatever is ... they're pragmatic and you know, all that stuff ... but when you get beneath that—that keeps changing because that's like a surface layer—you get beneath that, what do they think of america? Well they don't actually think america exists. i mean, i'm serious. It took me a long time to figure out that's how they were talking. They think this is one country, starting from about Guatemala and going up to the Canadian border. They think that's one country. Temporarily divided, from their point of view. These are manual laborers who didn't go to any university.

Their point of view is: It's only one country, that's why america has all these problems. America's denying that they're actually just one country with us down in Mexico. Because why? Well, we do all the work. How can they do without us? They say, look at the suburbs—this small business was in the suburbs— there's no white people working, there's no Asians working. Sorry, but it's true. The cooks at the pizza place, the cooks at the Thai restaurant, garbage collection, the domestics, construction laborers, even most delivery drivers, most of everything is Mexican, all the workers it feels like. They say, america really needs us. We don't quite understand this, their psychology, but you know those americans, they don't like to work. We will work and much of this country was ours anyway so actually it's just one country.

And they're not talking racially. One of the guys, his best friend married a Polish woman, immigrated from Poland. He said, "That's great, Mexicans and Poles, wonderful! Everyone should just get together!"

It isn't a racial thing to them. America as americans look at it is dysfunctional to them because it's based on a white society where most people don't work—in their terms "work" doesn't mean selling bonds or something, but laboring, meaning growing crops, busing the dishes, or whatever. This is a whole different thing to them.

So they're saying, they think essentially most of Mexico will move north and occupy much of what's presently the united states. Other people will come from all over the world, they see that happening, you know, like the Poles are coming over. Fine with them. And, you know, when americans give up their silly idea that they have this country called the united states, then we'll all live happily ever after.

These are guys from some peasant village in central Mexico. They don't come from the left. So, it's starting, but it's starting i think in part underground like all great movements start underground, where people don't see it, and i think it's developing in ways that we aren't going to anticipate, which often happens with things that masses of people just do. But i think desettlerizing has to happen because the whole idea that because in 1776 or something white people set up British colonies on the edge of this continent so america should be culturally and politically white is absurd as an idea. The ruling class, i understand why they're for that idea, but i don't think that's what's going to happen in the long run, and i don't mean a thousand years either. i think it's going to be a lot sooner than that.

END OF DISCUSSION

This is only a partial picture of the Q&A, since some of the questions and answers were too blurry on the recording to be transcribed.

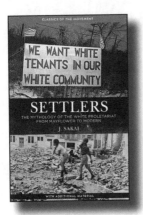

Settlers: The Mythology of the White Proletariat from Mayflower to Modern

J. Sakai • 978-1-62963-037-3
456 pages • $20.00

The United States is a country built on the theft of Indigenous lands and Afrikan labor, on the robbery of the northern third of Mexico, the colonization of Puerto Rico, and the expropriation of the Asian working class, with each of these crimes being accompanied by violence. In fact, America's white citizenry have never supported themselves but have always resorted to exploitation and theft, culminating in acts of genocide to maintain their culture and way of life. This movement classic lays it all out, taking us through this painful but important history.

This new edition includes "Cash & Genocide: The True Story of Japanese-American Reparations" and an interview with author J. Sakai by Ernesto Aguilar.

KERSPLEBEDEB, CP 63560, CCCP VAN HORNE, MONTREAL, QUEBEC, CANADA   H3W 3H8

ALSO AVAILABLE FROM KERSPLEBEDEB

**Basic Politics
of Movement Security
"A Talk on Security"
by J. Sakai &
"G20 Repression &
Infiltration
in Toronto:
An Interview with
Mandy Hiscocks"**

J. Sakai & Mandy Hiscocks
978-1-894946-52-0
72 pages • $7.00

*There are many books and articles reporting state repression,
but not on that subject's more intimate relative, movement
security. It is general practice to only pass along knowledge
about movement security privately, in closed group lectures
or by personal word-of-mouth. Adding to the confusion,
the handful of available left security texts are usually about
underground or illegal groups, not the far larger public
movements that work on a more or less legal level. Based
on their own personal experiences on this terrain, these two
"live" discussions by radical activists provide a partial remedy
to this situation.*

KERSPLEBEDEB, CP 63560, CCCP VAN HORNE, MONTREAL, QUEBEC, CANADA   H3W 3H8